HOW TO INVEST IN THE STOCK MARKET

Secrets Of The World's Best Stock Market Investors

By

Richard Nolan

Table of Contents

Introduction 4

Chapter 1 - Risk: Fear of Failure 8
    Discovering Your Investor Identity: Risk Tolerance ... 9
    Understanding Risk: Ignore the News 14

Chapter 2 - Active v Passive: Outsourcing 18
    Passive Investing: Choosing A Financial Advisor 20
    Exchange Traded Funds (ETFs) 24

Chapter 3 - Assets: Which to Choose? 28
    Asset Classes: Overview 28
    Equities 30
    Bonds 32
    Commodities 34
    Property 35
    Asset Classes: Risk Profiles 36

Chapter 4 - Equities: Mother of Markets 40
    Developed v Emerging Markets 45
    Market Sectors 46
    Market Capitalization 48
    ETF Variants 50

Chapter 5 - Bonds, Commodities & Property ... 53

Bonds 53
Credit Ratings 54
Government v Private Bonds 57
Bond ETFs 58
Commodities 60
Property 62

Chapter 6 - Valuation: EMH v Fundamentals 65
Fundamental Analysis 65
The Efficient Market Hypothesis (EMH) 69
Fundamental Analysis: Application 70

Chapter 7 - Alternative Investment Options 82
Volatility 83
Cryptocurrencies 85
Derivatives (Options & Futures) 87

Chapter 8 - Investment Strategies: Need to Know
.... 92
Diversification 92
Hedging 93
Portfolio Construction 94

Conclusion 101

Disclaimer 104

Introduction

Have you ever wanted to learn about investment? This is a topic shrouded in mystery and everywhere you turn, advice always appears to be given as a riddle. This book is different. We simplify the complex terminology and present ideas in a clear, practical manner. Beginners seek easy step-by-step guides and that is exactly what you will receive. We provide a chapter by chapter breakdown of key ideas and themes on investment, beginning with a discussion on what it is and why it is worth your time to learn about. Without realizing it, nearly everybody is somehow involved in the world of investment. Most workers have a pension and perhaps some savings; they are usually outsourced to a financial advisor who 'puts them to work' in the markets. If this applies to you, then your financial advisor or pension fund manager is actually investing your money on your behalf.

Each chapter is set out with simple lessons on investment that build on the knowledge discussed in the previous chapters. By the end of this book, you will discover how to assess your own tolerance to risk and gain clarity over your individual investor profile. Our recommendations will let you understand the key asset classes that exist for beginners and the best way to get started practically investing your money. We will introduce you to simple investment vehicles, known as ETFs and REITs, that can set you up managing your own investment portfolio regardless of your age and wealth objectives. Each chapter is then complemented by a summary of the Key Learning Points covered in that section.

Now that our roadmap is in place, let us turn our attention to the definition of investment. Firstly, what is investment? Investment is simply purchasing an item of value (known as an asset) with the intention of making money from it. This can either be through selling the same asset at a future time for more than you paid originally, or by receiving income from the asset over time. We can say that investment is centered on the idea of using money to make money. The challenge lies in choosing which asset to buy with your money; the guidance in this book is intended to prepare you to meet this challenge as you now begin your investor journey.

The second question you may want to be answered is why is learning about investment worthy of your time? This is a fair point. In a world where investment decisions can be outsourced, you may not feel that learning about investment is a priority. We have included a section on this way of thinking, known as passive investment. There are important tips here worth reading on how to select a financial advisor. However, if you are passionate to learn about the functions of the market, are capable of the intellectual challenge and do not wish to rely on somebody else to manage your money, then this book is for you. Are you still wondering why? How about this: money makes the world go around. Like it or not, this is a reality that you must face. Those that know how to manage their own money are better placed to succeed in this world. Fact. With that being said, let us not waste any more time... Welcome to the world of investment!

Chapter 1 - Risk: Fear of Failure

If you were to ask a member of the general public why they have never learned how to invest, you would be met by two predominant responses: "I don't know how" and "it's risky." Fear of not knowing is a common emotion; one that faces all of us. Nonetheless, this should never be a reason to outright cast aside opportunities for self-improvement. Learning to invest will give you access to skills that go far beyond simply improving your financial situation. Successful investing requires patience and self-discipline. It requires an ability to control your own self-doubts and the ability to ignore the views commonly put forward by the media that can cause panic in your investment strategy.

The first reason can be overcome by taking the plunge and reading meaningful advice from experts with practical experience; reading this book already puts you far ahead of most of the competition who have given up before ever trying. Meanwhile, the second reason that investing may be perceived as 'risky' is both a confusing and misconceived response. Isn't everything in life risky until you understand how it functions? Investment is no exception to this rule. In this chapter, we will look at the concept of risk in investment. We will tackle common misconceptions that put many people off investment and set you on a path of discovery to find out your own investor identity. Ready to start? Then, here we go...

Discovering Your Investor Identity: Risk Tolerance

A sensible starting point is to establish what we mean when we discuss risk in the context of investment. Most investors are excited by the possibilities that investing can bring - large upside wealth potential. Yet, there is an equal counterweight to the benefits. When investors talk about risk, they are explaining their desire to avoid losing the amount of money that they have invested in the market. As market prices fluctuate, portfolio returns can be both positive and negative. The risk of investing is, therefore, the likelihood of losing part or all of your initial invested sum of money - known as your principle or initial capital. When you understand this point, it becomes clear why saying that "investing is risky" is really a meaningless statement. The likelihood of losing your initial capital is dependent upon a number of key factors: your investing strategy, your portfolio asset allocation and your investing time horizon being three of the most important. So, how can you determine what level of risk you will be exposing yourself to when you first start out investing and equally as important, how can you mitigate that risk?

All investors may assign themselves a level of risk tolerance that forms the base of their investor identity. No doubt when asked what level of risk you are willing to accept, an answer immediately comes to mind. Risk tolerance is a trait that often goes hand-in-hand with your personality. If you are timid by nature, you may consider yourself risk-averse. Otherwise, less introvert people may be rather risk-neutral. Meanwhile, at the other end of the spectrum, the extrovert characters may actively seek out risk - these are the risk-takers. Determining your own risk tolerance is an essential exercise as it shall shape many of your future investing decisions as you proceed through the coming chapters.

Your age and wealth objectives are the two most important components that can direct clarity to deciding your risk tolerance. If you are new to the career ladder, perhaps in your 20s or 30s, your main wealth objective is likely to make as much money as possible as quickly as possible. This is an understandable position to be in and is a perfectly legitimate position to take in investing. This would tend to lean you towards a risk-taker mindset, however this does come with strings attached. With the potential to make more money in a faster timeframe, your initial capital will be exposed to larger potential downside swings. This means that as you take more risk in investing, the likelihood of losing your original investment increases. Risk and reward are two sides of the same coin; greater potential reward entails greater risk.

If, instead, you find yourself in your midlife - say in your 40s and 50s - your wealth objectives are likely very different from those of your younger counterparts. You may be willing to forego large upside potential for increased safety. Instead of looking for rapid wealth expansion, you may have savings that you wish to grow while minimizing the chance of experiencing losses. You may have children whose education will need funding and your attention may be looking to retirement as it is approaching over the near horizon. These circumstances would place you in a risk-neutral category. Your investing strategy will expose you to a limited level of risk as you look to grow your savings at a steady pace over time.

The final risk tolerance level is saved for the risk-averse. If you are already retired, then this is likely your comfort zone. By older age, your wealth objectives will no longer be looking to grow your wealth but rather, to preserve it. Maximizing income to support a comfortable retirement is the desired outcome for this group. It makes logical sense to minimize the risk of losses at this point as without the support of alternative income sources, losses become far more meaningful. Whereas, those at working age may mitigate their investment losses by generating more savings from their day job. This option is not available for retirees.

From these three levels of risk tolerance, we can now see why one is never better or worse than another. It is specific to your individual wealth objectives, which change as you age. Take the time to consider the points raised here and decide on your own category. What is your risk tolerance level? Remember your answer and place it at the heart of your new investor identity!

Understanding Risk: Ignore the News

We live in an age that is driven by information and the media. Although the advancement of technology and the pioneering developments of the internet have made us more connected than ever before, this has not necessarily been a productive occurrence for those starting out in the world of investment. The world of investment is filled with practitioners of many different approaches, some of whom disagree with each other. Naturally, this can prove hazardous if you are easily led astray by the next new, exciting technique that 'professionals' on the news may support. The latest trend revolves around cryptocurrencies, which we shall come back to explore in more detail. Social media and news outlets are ablaze with advertisements inviting beginners to try their luck with this latest investment option. No! As a beginner, you must develop self-assurance and remind yourself that not all new investment options will be suitable for your own risk tolerance. Learn to cast aside unhelpful advice; in the long run, this will serve you well.

A common dictum of the investment world is to buy low and sell high. In principle, this is clearly good advice - albeit somewhat self-explanatory. So why is it that the average investor is unable to put this simple solution into practice? Emotions. Successful investing relies on developing a rational strategy that has been shown to yield good results in the past. This is precisely why you must learn to ignore the news of 'financial experts' and in doing so, develop a consistent investment approach. The majority of new investors have no clear understanding of how their portfolio is distributed between assets and the reasons for this allocation. Some may even prefer to outsource the decision entirely to a financial advisor or a pension fund. However, by following the crowd in this manner it is possible that you will subject yourself to doing the precise opposite of good investment behavior: selling low and buying high.

If you are wondering how to avoid this disaster, then do not panic. I shall repeat that: do not panic! Fear is the enemy of investors that lack guidance. Yet, it can be a powerful friend for those in the know. When an apparent expert - be it a financial advisor, banker or economist - goes on the news and warns that the market could collapse, new investors may be tempted to listen to that advice. They rush to sell their assets and cause the market price to go lower. The more people that listen to this advice, the faster the prophecy is fulfilled. In other words, the market can go lower just by people believing that it will go lower. Meanwhile, investors who are able to remain composed see this selling frenzy as a buying opportunity. They are able to swim against the tide as they have developed self-discipline. The chapters that follow will help you to develop this much-needed skill by setting out a clear investment approach to match your risk tolerance. Once you have mastered the basics, you will then possess the confidence to ignore the crowd and find money-making opportunities while the majority panic and sell their assets at unfavorable prices.

Key Learning Points

- Risk in investment is the likelihood of losing part or all of your initial capital
- Risk and reward are two sides to the same coin
- Your risk tolerance is determined by your age and wealth objectives
- Identify your own risk tolerance; are you a risk-taker, risk-neutral or risk-averse?
- Your own emotions can tempt you into poor investment decisions
- Learn to ignore the actions of the crowd; trust your own investment strategy
- Look for panic selling in the market as a good opportunity to buy cheap assets

Chapter 2 - Active v Passive: Outsourcing

Now that you have a clearer idea of your own risk tolerance, we can begin to build on a second trait of your investor identity: do you want to be an active or passive investor? Active investing is the DIY of the investing world. This approach is a time-intensive means to managing your own investment portfolio in detail. The benefit is that you will gain first-hand experience of how to pick your own asset allocation, making you proactive rather than reactive. Active investing is our recommended path if you have the self-discipline to learn from your own mistakes, improving your investing skillset with time. An active investor performs his/her own research and selects which individual companies or assets to buy and sell. Although beginners may seek shortcuts to the advice throughout this book, no better way exists to learning than through experience. As an active investor, you should begin your investing journey with a small proportion of your savings. Take the time to build up your knowledge as your competence increases and you can slowly add more of your savings into new assets as you become more confident in the markets.

The alternative option is passive investing. This is otherwise known as outsourcing. If you are pressured by time constraints or you do not possess the desire to spend considerable time learning the skills required to become a sophisticated investor, then this may be your best option. Rather than ignoring investment as a topic all together, passive investing allows a financial expert to determine the most appropriate investment approach for your circumstances. The main problem with this selection is that it exposes naïve individuals to being exploited if they do not perform due diligence in their selection. All the same, there is no need to worry as many competent advisors do exist that will charge you reasonably for their services. We shall examine the common pitfalls to consider if you are looking to choose a financial advisor whom you may trust with managing your money.

Passive Investing: Choosing A Financial Advisor

When seeking a financial advisor to manage your investment portfolio on your behalf, you will be overwhelmed by available options. The internet is full of advertisements from investment funds and individuals who are eager to attract your money. Before you get in contact and begin receiving a sales pitch that is designed to convince you to sign over your money, consider the following step-by-step plan that will allow you to make an informed decision.

Research at least three different options with accredited advisors

If you know of family or friends that already have a trusted financial advisor, then consider having them put you in contact. All financial advisors must be accredited with the relevant government regulatory body to ensure that they are eligible to provide investment advice. Request these credentials before any discussion with a potential advisor and independently check them with the regulatory body in your country. An internet search should inform you of the relevant regulatory body in your country.

Once you are sure of the legitimacy of your potential advisor's accreditation, you should always find out the full scope of charges and have the advisor present you with their track record of returns before contemplating handing over your savings. By giving yourself a comparison of at least three options, you will get a better understanding of which advisors are charging reasonable rates to manage your money.

Ask your potential advisor to demonstrate their ability

No advisor worthy of your money should shy away from proving their investing ability to you. Ask to see a track record of their average returns over the last 5 to 10 years. You can then compare these average returns to the market benchmark (the average market return over the same time period) to see if your potential advisor is really able to add value to your investments.

Keep in mind that the advisor with the highest returns may not necessarily be your best selection. As you have already discovered, risk and return have a trade-off between them. Ask to understand the asset allocations that the potential advisor would recommend for your circumstances. With the knowledge that you will receive in future chapters, you will be well positioned to understand if the recommended portfolio seems appropriate for your own risk tolerance and investor identity.

Compare advisors and make an informed decision

Once you are comfortable with the answers that you have received from the previous two steps, you can make an informed choice. Your new advisor should arrange a face-to-face meeting with you to understand your financial situation, wealth objectives and risk tolerance. These factors will then enable the advisor to propose an asset allocation for your portfolio that is tailored to your circumstances.

If unhappy with your original selection, change advisor

The markets can fluctuate in the short run, though the trend is always upwards over time. Keep this in mind so that you do not judge your advisor's investment approach too harshly if you see poor results in the very beginning. You should ask your advisor for quarterly investment updates (a record of your investment performance every 3 months). This return figure can then be compared to the market benchmark to see how your portfolio has performed compared to the average market return in the same time period.

Remember that you can always change financial advisor if your returns are not meeting your expectations. You pay a management fee to your investment advisor (anything between 1-2% can be reasonable by industry standards) so if you feel that he/she is mismanaging your savings, take them elsewhere. You can restart the selection process as set out in these steps until you find an advisor that is investing your money for your benefit.

Exchange Traded Funds (ETFs)

There are investment vehicles that allow a passive investor to make a step towards becoming an active investor. One of these is known as the Exchange Traded Fund (ETF). These have become very popular in the modern investing scene, with large pension funds and investment institutions recommending them for beginning investors. These are funds that are designed to track the average return of a basket of companies. Their versatility is their main selling point as the common thread between each of the companies in the basket can vary by sector, size and country. That means that if you are an interested in agricultural companies, as an example, ETFs exist for this option that you may invest in without having to be an expert on selecting which individual agricultural companies to choose. Instead, the ETF's return is designed to mimic the average return of the agricultural sector in this example.

As a new investor, ETFs are a great way to present you with a learning opportunity while investing your own money from the outset. Many of the skills that you will require as you progress to more sophisticated investment are the same as those taught by selecting ETFs that match your interests. Each ETF has an investment provider, the company that has structured the basket, who publishes a dedicated information page for that ETF on their website. By searching for ETFs in a sector that matches your interests, take the US technology sector as an example, you can use this information page to research the track record of the ETF's past investment returns, the investment fee that the provider charges for investing in the fund and the composition of the companies in the fund itself.

You can even take your research efforts one step further and compare available ETFs that track the same sector. Different providers exist on the market that will charge their own investment fee. If you are most interested in selecting a reliable provider that charges the lowest fee, this can be found by performing a simple comparison by ETF provider. All major search engines generate these lists. As an example of this point, type in 'US Technology ETFs' to your internet search engine and you will immediately be presented with databases that track the total assets invested in each technology sector ETF for the US. We would recommend that you stick to the ETFs with the most assets being managed while learning as the fees are usually most reasonable for these large ETF providers.

Key Learning Points

- Decide if you wish to be an active or passive investor
- Active investing is the DIY approach; passive investing is outsourcing to a financial advisor
- Always perform due diligence when selecting a financial advisor - our step-by-step approach will allow you to avoid the common pitfalls
- ETFs are a great option for passive investors who wish to tip their toe in the world of active investing; they are versatile and track the average investment return of a basket of companies by market sector, size or country
- ETFs can be researched and compared by investment fee, assets under management and company composition

Chapter 3 - Assets: Which to Choose?

In this chapter, we look at the potential investment options available for your money. So, first things first, what exactly is an asset? An asset is simply an item of value; one that can be purchased with your savings and is expected to be worth more to the investor in the future. Investment is centered around establishing a portfolio of these assets. There are varying types of assets, each with their own unique investment traits that lend themselves better to differing risk tolerances, wealth objectives and time horizons. We shall explore these major asset types in turn and recommend which are best suited to a novice investor.

Asset Classes: Overview

The main asset types are split into equities, bonds, commodities and property. These categories are large and encompass numerous forms of each. One main consideration between each broad selection is whether or not the asset type can be considered productive or non-productive. Let us first consider that when an investor buys an asset, he/she seeks to make money over time in one of two ways:

- The asset value itself increases in price - known as a capital gain
- The asset generates an income for the investor

While all assets can allow the investor to make money through changes in the market price, not all assets generate an income. Assets with the second attribute are referred to as productive, while assets that do not produce an income are deemed non-productive.

Some short-term traders, commonly known as speculators, look to buy assets and sell them back to the market at a better price in a short time period. This behavior is separate from investment as we define it in this book as it focuses on a short time horizon. This is more akin to gambling than investing and is beyond the scope of our discussion. Instead, investors should look to establish a portfolio of different assets (known as asset allocation) that match their wealth objectives and allow time to work in their favor for those assets to generate capital gains and income.

Equities

The best-known asset class in the world of investment are shares, otherwise known as equities. These were once issued as stock certificates in paper but are predominantly maintained electronically now by your investment broker. These are symbolic proportions of a business that entitle the investor to a share of the profits made by that company. While shares can be bought in any company, private or public, the shares that are listed on the stock market are all equities in publicly-listed companies. The reasons why a company may choose to issue shares to the market are complicated but the most significant justification is that it provides a means of raising funds for the firm. In exchange for these funds, investors can make capital gains or income (known as dividends) from their shares.

Each financial year, publicly-listed companies must declare their net profit figure. This is the total amount of money that the company has earned in that financial year after deducting all expenses, including paying down any debt interest that the company may owe to its bondholders. Shareholders are then entitled to a proportionate share of these profits, depending on the number of shares that the investor owns. The company may either choose to retain these profits within the business, reinvesting them to promote future growth of the company, or pay the shareholders the profits in cash - known as making a dividend payment. Dividends are simply a distribution of profits that a company has earned to its shareholders/investors. If a company retains its earnings and invests them efficiently to increase its ability to earn more profits in the future, the value of the overall company should increase. This, in turn, should be reflected in the market price of the shares; this capital gain is the first way that an investor may make money with equities. The second method is through dividend payments, which are a form of income for investors. Therefore, equities are productive assets.

Bonds

Bonds are issued both by the government and private businesses as a means to raise funds in the form of debt. Unlike issuing shares, this way of raising funds does not give away any ownership (equity) in the business. Instead, the bondholders give their money over in good faith that the amount invested will be returned to them at the end of the bond duration. In the meantime, bondholders are compensated each year with an annual coupon or interest payment from the bond issuer. For instance, if a bond is issued by the US government for a duration of 10 years at an interest rate of 5%, a bondholder may invest $1,000 in that bond. Each year, the bondholder expects to receive an interest payment of 5% - or $50 - of the amount invested. Then, at the end of the 10 years, the government will return the original $1,000 (the principle) investment back to the bondholder.

As bonds offer the possibility both for capital gains and income, they too are deemed productive assets. An important relationship for all investors to understand with bonds is that their market price moves inversely to movements in the interest base rate. All major economies are governed by a central bank - in the US, this is the Federal Reserve (the Fed). This body is responsible for measuring and controlling the inflation rate in the economy. If this rate goes too high, then the real value of the economy's currency can be devalued. Bondholders need to be aware of this fact as the base interest rate set by the central bank impacts the prices in the bond market. An increase in this interest rate will mean that bond prices in general will decrease. Precisely why this relationship exists will be covered later in the book. For now, it is simply a noteworthy point to keep in mind as a new investor considering bonds as an asset class.

Commodities

Commodities are raw materials that trade on their own market and can be deemed homogenous - that being that one item is not materially different in quality to another. Examples include metals such as gold and silver, agricultural products such as wheat and corn, meat products and so forth. These goods can fluctuate substantially in price due to supply chain developments and weather conditions. In addition, unlike the other major asset classes, commodities do not produce an income for their investors - they are non-productive assets. Due to this unique trait, these markets are often deemed more appropriate for sophisticated investors and speculators who look to take advantage of fast price movements. Nonetheless, they may have their place in the portfolio of beginner and intermediate investors who take the time to understand how their markets function.

Property

Property makes up the last major asset class and can be divided into residential and commercial property. The first subcategory relates to properties that are owned by individuals who use them as their place of residence, while the second subcategory relates to locations used by businesses such as malls. This is a productive asset as property values fluctuate, as well as providing income in the form of rent to the owner. Although directly owning property can be an expensive investment option, investment vehicles exist known as Real Estate Investment Trusts (REITs) that follow the same principles of ETFs. These are effectively baskets of different real estate shares that allow investors to track the performance of property prices without outright owning the property itself. This can be an interesting addition to a beginning investor's portfolio.

Asset Classes: Risk Profiles

Now that we have covered the main asset classes available to you as a new investor, it is worthwhile discussing which are most suitable for your risk tolerance level. Remember back to this principle as it is now going to help you determine which asset classes to choose when first putting together your portfolio.

Equities are a staple component of all portfolios. They should, however, be perceived as having a medium to high level of risk as individual companies in different sectors always face the possibility of bad business news causing their share price to fall. That is why an ETF may be a more suitable substitute for starting out with equities as a basket of shares made up of multiple companies is less likely to be affected by bad news for one company amongst many. Equities are therefore an appropriate selection for all investors, yet they are best suited for the risk-neutral and risk-takers.

Bonds are known for being a very reliable investment option. Unlike equity prices, which can be impacted by business-specific news, the main driver of bond prices is simply the central bank's base rate. We should point out that bonds issued by private companies are affected by business-specific news, however risk-averse investors can avoid this issue by sticking to bonds issued by governments of large economies. The interest rate for these bonds is lower than their counterparts issued in the private sector, but this reflects the lower risk of the government going bankrupt rather than a private company.

Commodities are arguably the asset class with the most embedded risk. They are non-productive assets that are favored by speculators. Beginners would be well advised to avoid this asset class, but intermediate investors with a risk-seeking approach for large potential upside could consider them for a small percentage of their overall portfolio's asset allocation.

Property REITs are a nice addition to complement a well-balanced portfolio. These are similar in function to ETFs and as such, it is easy for a beginning investor to advance his/her understanding from equities to property through this investment vehicle. Property is best suited to risk-averse and risk-neutral investors as it provides small potential capital gains over time and brings in regular rental income.

Key Learning Points

- Productive assets generate capital gains and an income for the investor; non-productive assets do not generate an income
- Speculators look to exploit price changes in the short term; investors look to accumulate

wealth through their asset allocation in the long term
- The main asset classes are equities, bonds, commodities and property
- Bond prices move inversely with movements in the central bank's base interest rate
- Risk-averse investors should consider investing in bonds and property
- Risk-neutral investors should consider investing in equities and bonds
- Risk-seeking investors should consider investing in equities and commodities

Chapter 4 - Equities: Mother of Markets

You have already been introduced to equities as an asset class. Here we explore the market in detail so that you may understand why companies issue shares to the market and how it benefits investors to trade those shares.

Public companies may look to fund their operations through two main options: debt and equity. The benefits of using debt will be explored in a later chapter. Once a firm decides that it will use equity as its funding source, it effectively agrees to sell part of the ownership in the company to investors in return for funds to grow its operations. This method of expanding companies has allowed the growth of multinational corporations around the globe. Participants in the stock market collectively have vast amounts of wealth available to invest in worthy companies. Companies, therefore, benefit when issuing shares as it grants them access to this extensive source of funding. We have provided a simplified overview of this process below.

- A company must first become publicly listed on a stock market to issue shares; this entails strict regulatory checks and regular reporting requirements so that investors may analyze the finances of the company on a quarterly basis. The company must also produce a detailed Annual Report each financial year which summarizes its operational performance.
- The company decides to raise funds by issuing shares.
- The company may either privately offer these shares for sale to large institutional investors (pension funds and investment banks) or offer the shares for direct sale to the public through an initial public offering (IPO).
- Investors will be informed of the IPO date and a valuation price will be assigned to each share as the starting trading price.
- Once the shares begin trading, the market price will fluctuate up and down depending on investor demand. The more buyers, the higher the share price will go. The more sellers, the lower the share price will fall.
- Going forward, the share price will be allowed to fluctuate depending on the fortunes of the

company. The better the company performs, the higher the share price will rise.
- If the company ever decides to raise more funds by issuing shares, it must accept the share price that the market has now set. This explains why it is in a company's interest for its own share price to be high.

By understanding the process behind a company issuing shares, you should now have a better idea of how it benefits firms to list their shares on the stock market. However, as an investor who is interested in the equity asset class, how exactly do you buy or sell shares? It is a common misconception for new investors that you buy or sell shares directly with the company that interests you. In fact, as we have discussed, it is a rare occurrence for companies to issue shares to the market. In most cases, investors are actually buying and selling shares with each other. So, while you may think that it is a great time to invest in a company by buying its shares, there is equally another investor in the world who has decided to sell you those shares. This is always worth keeping in mind as investment is a competitive field. It should not scare you away from investment as all markets require an equal number of buyers and sellers to function, however it is yet another example of how self-discipline is required to pursue your own investment strategy regardless of what other investors are doing around you.

You should already be familiar with equities as productive assets. It is your intention when buying shares through your investment broker to increase your wealth through capital appreciation (increases in the share price) and through dividend payments - which are a distribution of the company's profits to its shareholders. When you wish to recognize this gain in the future, you will sell your shares at a higher price than you originally paid. A more sophisticated investment strategy exists that you should be aware of, though it is not suitable for beginners. Short selling is where an investor borrows shares that he/she does not own and sells them to the market with the expectation that the share price will fall. If the share price does fall, the investor will buy back the shares on the market at the lower price and return them to the original owner. This means that short selling can allow sophisticated investors to make money when the share price decreases.

We have previously mentioned the rise in popularity of Exchange Traded Funds (ETFs). These present a new investor with an affordable way to track the return of multiple companies. Instead of buying shares in an individual company, you can choose to buy shares in an ETF that interests you. These ETFs are versatile and are comprised of equities from stock markets all over the world. In order to give you a better idea of what to look for when investing in your first ETFs, we will explore some of the most popular options.

Developed v Emerging Markets

ETFs exist that focus on the difference between developed and emerging markets. Developed market ETFs are comprised of companies that operate and are listed on the stock markets of stable, richer economies in the world. These could be companies listed on the US or European stock markets as an example. Contrarily, emerging market ETFs are formed of companies that operate in rapidly expanding economies that are on their way to becoming developed economies. These economies are often undergoing rapid industrialization, with South East Asian companies being an often-cited example.

Investors may spread their portfolio between developed and emerging economies in this way as a means of diversifying their returns. While developed economies are more reliable, with less perceived risk of bankruptcy for their companies, the growth rates are also lower. Investors with a larger appetite for risk could, therefore, consider emerging market ETFs to capture the higher growth rates of these economies, while taking on the additional exposure that some of the companies in these less stable areas may go bankrupt.

Market Sectors

ETFs are not only confined to companies in different economies around the globe, they can also be segregated by market sectors. These ETFs look to form a basket of companies that are all related to a particular activity within the economy, thereby tracking the performance of that specific market sector. We have listed the main market sectors below for your consideration:

Financials - banks, investment funds and insurance companies

Utilities - electric, gas and water suppliers

Consumer Discretionary - retail and luxury consumer purchases

Consumer Staples - necessity consumer purchases e.g. supermarkets

Energy - predominantly oil and gas companies

Healthcare - biotech and medical suppliers

Industrials - aerospace, defense and manufacturing firms

Technology - software and hardware firms

Telecommunications - internet and telephone providers

Materials - mining and raw material providers

Investors should be careful not to weight their portfolio too heavily towards one market sector. Each market sector reacts differently to changes in the economic cycle. For instance, Consumer Discretionary companies are likely to suffer in a recession and will increase in conditions of strong economic growth. Meanwhile, Consumer Staples revolve around goods that consumers must buy regardless of overall economic conditions. This is perceived as a safer market sector that will not experience large growth but should generate stable returns over time. As a new investor, you should reflect on your own risk-tolerance and seek out market sector ETFs that are appropriate for your own wealth objectives.

Market Capitalization

When a company first lists on the stock market, it is assigned a market capitalization. This is the total value of the company, calculated by multiplying the share price by the number of shares issued by the firm. As each company is then given a market cap, ETFs can be formed of companies based on size. The four main categories of company size are listed below:

Micro-cap: companies with a value between $50 - $300 million USD

Small-cap: companies with a value between $300 million - $2 billion USD

Mid-cap: companies with a value between $2 billion - $10 billion USD

Large-cap: companies with a value over $10 billion USD

A simple rule of thumb is that smaller companies are perceived to have the highest risk of bankruptcy as they have less access to funding and poor operational decisions can lead them to financial ruin. Meanwhile, the largest companies are well-established with global customer bases and often have large cash reserves to weather the storm of poor operational decisions. We once again observe a trade-off between risk and reward. Investors with a risk-averse attitude would be well advised to stick to large-cap ETFs, while risk-seeking investors can hope to achieve larger returns in the micro-cap ETFs. Smaller companies are able to grow faster than larger companies which means that the micro and small-cap ETFs are expected to achieve a higher average return for investors, while exposing them to more risk.

ETF Variants

During your research of ETFs, you will likely come across a few variants that we have not yet mentioned. We examine these ETFs here to present you with an overview of the possibilities available on the market. However, you should recognize that these variants can expose the investor to larger risk and are more appropriate for sophisticated investors.

Leveraged ETFs have become popular in the last decade as offering up to 2x or 3x returns. Leverage is another way of saying debt. These ETFs aim to offer investors enhanced returns by employing debt. However, not all is as good as it appears. These ETFs work both ways; gains and losses are multiplied. Although they can present investors with increased returns when the market acts favorably, they also expose investors to greater risk of losses. For this reason, we would suggest that beginners are made aware of them but should not incorporate them in their investment approach. These products are best left to speculators.

One variant of ETF that has emerged may be of interest to some beginning investors. Instead of just selecting one category, such as developed or emerging markets, you may be interested to combine these choices. ETFs exist that focus on company size and location. An example could be a small-cap emerging markets ETF. These combinations display the versatility of ETFs which is why they have become so popular in the investing community. New investors may form a portfolio of ETFs which diversifies between geographical location, market sector and company size. These combinations are vast and serve all wealth objectives when selected appropriately.

Key Learning Points

- Companies issue shares on the stock market by selling equity (ownership) in their company in return for investor funding
- A share gives the investor the right to receive a proportion of the company's profits in the form of dividends
- Equities are productive assets that allow the investor to gain through capital appreciation (share price increases) and income (in the form of dividends)
- ETFs are a great addition to a beginner's portfolio as they provide exposure to a basket of companies, not just an individual firm
- ETFs can categorize businesses by geographical location, market sector and market capitalization; adventurous investors can even combine these options

Chapter 5 - Bonds, Commodities & Property

Bonds

We have already examined the reasons why a company may choose to fund its operations through issuing shares, here we turn our attention to debt funding. The first reason that a company would choose to use debt rather than equity as its principle funding method is that the firm may not wish to sell the rights to its profits. Bondholders, unlike shareholders, only have the right to be paid back their original investment (the face value of the bond) at the end of the bond's duration and any interest payments promised as per the terms of the bond. Bondholders are not entitled to a distribution of the profits that a company earns. Therefore, if a company is highly profitable, selling its own equity may not be a sensible strategic option as those profits would be better retained and distributed amongst existing shareholders.

Credit Ratings

All entities, private and public, that are authorized to issue bonds are given a credit rating by the leading global credit rating agencies (CRAs). Two of the best known CRAs are Standard and Poor's (S&P), and Moody's. Their purpose is to provide an independent rating to issuers of bonds so that investors may know what risk they are taking on when purchasing these bonds. If a bond issuer goes bankrupt then it is forced to default on its bond interest payments, as well as not returning the principal investment to the bondholders. This is the main risk that bondholders accept when investing in this asset class.

The CRAs each use their own scale of credit ratings, but they are broadly similar. We shall illustrate this scale using the ratings issued by S&P.

Investment Grade Bonds

AAA

AA+, AA, AA-

A+, A, A-

BBB+, BBB, BBB-

Non-Investment Grade Bonds (Junk Bonds)

BB+, BB, BB-

B+, B, B-

CCC+, CCC, CCC-

CC

C

D - in default

You will notice that credit ratings go from AAA rated as the highest quality, all the way down to D, which means that the bond issuer is in default (i.e. it has failed to make an interest payment to its bondholders). These ratings are further separated into investment grade and non-investment grade. Within the investment industry, investment grade bonds are considered the least likely to default on interest payments, whereas the non-investment grade bonds come with a certain expectation that the bond issuers may default. This has led to non-investment grade bonds being known more colloquially as 'junk bonds.'

Given the choice of investment grade bonds, why then would an investor ever choose to invest in a company with a poor credit rating? The answer is that lower grade bonds offer higher interest rates to tempt investors. Bondholders must understand that if they take on the additional risk of lower credit rated bonds, they will receive higher interest payments but expose their original investment to being lost if the company goes bankrupt. In order to apply this new knowledge to your own investor identity, risk-averse investors should stick to investment grade bonds only and risk-seekers may desire to enhance their returns with junk bonds but should recognize the risk that this involves before doing so.

Government v Private Bonds

It is important to denote a distinction between government and private bonds. Our discussion up until this point has focused on bonds issued by private companies. However, national governments also issue bonds to raise funds for public projects such as infrastructure spending. In a similar fashion to private companies, national governments are also assigned a credit rating. The developed economies of the world are given the highest credit ratings, while developing economies with more political risk are assigned lower ratings. As an example, bonds issued by the US government have the highest credit rating - AAA. However, as the likelihood of the US government defaulting on its interest payments is practically nil, the interest rate of these bonds is one of the lowest available in the bond market.

The US government issues bonds for durations from 3 months up to 30 years. The further out in time the bond is issued for, the higher the interest rate given on the bond. This is an important relationship to understand for new bondholders. All bondholders recognize that the predominant risk of this asset class is not receiving the principle investment back at the end of the bond duration. The faster that this amount is returned, the less risk is involved. This is the justification for why shorter duration bonds pay on average a lower interest rate than longer duration bonds. The longer the duration of the bond, the more risk involved for the bondholder that he/she may not receive the principle back - the higher interest rate compensates for this increased risk.

Bond ETFs

Now that you understand the principles behind sensible bond investing, how can you start investing? Once again, ETFs provide new investors with a useful answer. As a smaller investor - known as a retail investor - you are unable to buy most bonds directly from public companies, though you may be able to buy certain bonds from your national government. Instead, bond ETFs have been formed as a basket of bonds that are already owned by larger investment providers. These are categorized by investment grade bonds or junk bond ETFs (also named high-yield bond ETFs). By researching the ETF information page, you will be able to see the percentage composition of bonds held within the ETF by credit rating.

We would recommend that new investors should stick to ETFs filled with investment grade bonds only. The risks of default associated with junk bond ETFs make them better suited to sophisticated investors. You should also realize that investing in a bond ETF is not the same as outright owning a bond. By investing in a bond ETF, you will become the owner of shares in that fund which tracks the price movements of the bonds and pays out interest payments. However, this differs from owning a bond outright as you will not receive a principle payment from a bond ETF. The durations of the bonds in the ETF will continually vary and as old bonds expire, the fund will reinvest the principle into new bonds to continue the process for future investors.

Commodities

One of the alternative asset classes to equities and bonds are commodities. These can be subdivided into soft and hard commodities. Soft commodities - known to commodity traders as the 'softs' - are commodities that are grown, rather than mined. Meanwhile, hard commodities are sourced from the ground - these are principally raw materials and precious metals.

The main categories of soft commodities include coffee, cocoa, sugar, cotton, corn, wheat, soybeans, fruits and livestock. Contrarily, the main categories of hard commodities include precious metals (gold, silver, palladium and platinum), industrial materials (copper, lead, tin, aluminum, etc.), energy (natural gas, heating oil, crude oil, ethanol, etc.) and others (rubber, palm oil and more). As can be seen from these lists, the number of commodities of each type is extensive. Furthermore, each individual commodity has its own dedicated market that reacts to industry news and events. This can be an overwhelming prospect for new investors and is why we would recommend getting comfortable with the other asset classes before turning your attention to commodities.

That warning said, some commodities can add an interesting element of diversification to your asset allocation. As all commodities are non-productive assets, gains are made in these markets through capital appreciation alone. Unless you consider yourself an expert on one particular commodity, which few novice investors will, then you could consider investing in an ETF made up of many commodities. For example, precious metal ETFs - which track the prices of gold, silver, platinum and palladium - often move independently to the stock and bond markets. This is the basis for a well-diversified portfolio, as we will explore in a later chapter. The key takeaway of commodities as an asset class is that they lend themselves better to speculation than long term investment, as their prices can fluctuate dramatically. This means that investors increase their risk of losses with this asset class. In the case of a new investor, commodities should be added as a small component of a balanced portfolio rather than form the main asset class of your investment approach.

Property

The final major asset class is property. We have already considered that this can be further separated into residential and commercial property. Real Estate Investment Trusts (REITs) provide the most practical means for a retail investor to track property prices of either type. Similarly to bonds, investing in a REIT does have similar features to owning property outright but it is not entirely the same. Firstly, investing into a REIT will make you the owner of shares in the fund. You will not be the owner of property but rather the proportional owner of a fund that tracks a basket of property values. Property is a productive asset that lends itself well to risk-averse and risk-neutral investors. REITs will give you exposure to price changes in the underlying properties and pay out dividends for the rent collected. The property market, both residential and commercial, has always been associated as a stable investment choice. There is limited upside potential with this investment choice, however the steady income stream that it provides makes it a useful addition to the portfolio of retirees and those approaching retirement.

Key Learning Points

- Bondholders are entitled to interest payments for the duration of the bond and the return of the principle (the bond face value) at the end of this duration
- Bondholders are not entitled to a share of the company's profits
- All issuers of bonds are assigned an independent credit rating; bond issuers can be assigned an investment grade or non-investment grade rating from AAA down to D
- Risk-averse investors should only invest in bond ETFs that focus on investment grade bonds
- The longer the duration of the bond, the higher the average interest rate
- Commodities are a non-productive asset class that are better suited to intermediate investors with a high-risk appetite
- Property is an asset class that lends itself well to retirees and those approaching retirement

Chapter 6 - Valuation: EMH v Fundamentals

In this chapter, we will look at an important underlying theoretical debate that is taking place in the world of investment. Although you may not consider the theory of particular relevance, the context that it will provide should prove invaluable to your ability to make investment decisions. This discussion lies at the heart of your investment approach and it takes place between the Efficient Market Hypothesis (EMH) and fundamental analysis. These are two of the modern academic approaches to the valuation of assets, specifically focusing on equities.

Fundamental Analysis

We begin with fundamental analysis, which is a school of thought that encourages researching the financial situation of firms in order to estimate a value for the entire company - this is referred to as the intrinsic value. This total value can then be calculated on a per share basis by dividing the valuation of the firm by the total number of shares issued. If the market share price is below this intrinsic value per share, the shares should be bought as they are undervalued according to this approach. Alternatively, if the share price is above the intrinsic value per share, then investors should sell their shares. The theory is based on a central belief that the market share price will converge towards the intrinsic value per share over time.

The main advantage of fundamental analysis is that it suggests investor research can be benefited by economic reward. While beginner investors are able to stick to ETFs which track the average market return, fundamental analysis is a more sophisticated investment approach that aims to find undervalued companies in which to invest. The hope being that this approach can then generate investment returns that beat the average market return. Various studies have attempted to refute and prove this claim to no conclusive finding. In principle, this theoretical approach does hold some merit. ETFs are baskets of companies based on size, market sector or geographical location; they do not distinguish by undervalued and overvalued companies. If an investor is, therefore, able to select companies based on their financial performance, as opposed to a simple metric such as size alone, then it may stand to reason that this investor places himself/herself in a position to make above average market returns.

There are, however, clear challenges posed by this investment approach in theory and practice. One major critique is that estimates of intrinsic value for the same company can vary greatly depending on the investor performing the calculations. This creates a large margin of error which makes comparison between the intrinsic value estimate and the share price challenging when applied. In addition, companies release an Annual Report of their financial statements each financial year. The amount of data in these reports is staggering, not to mention that the information is presented in both quantitative and qualitative forms. Fundamental analysis gives far more importance to factors that can be quantified, which means that much of the important qualitative information - including key operational decisions - is ignored within this approach.

We shall return to some of the simpler practical tools that investors are presented with through the fundamental analysis school of thought. However, we have decided to leave it up to you to decide which school of thought you prefer. As academics have still not conclusively demonstrated one approach over the other, this is currently a matter of investor choice. If you decide to adopt fundamental analysis into your investment approach, you may have a stronger basis for investing in individual companies but beginners may prefer to stick to the less time-consuming method of investing in ETFs. The ongoing theoretical debate demonstrates that the world of investment is still developing in the modern day.

The Efficient Market Hypothesis (EMH)

The Efficient Market Hypothesis (EMH) is a central pillar of modern financial theory, though it is widely disputed by proponents of fundamental analysis. It effectively states that researching companies based on their financial statements is a waste of time because market prices react so quickly to news events that investors cannot take advantage of under or overvaluation. The theory being that all financial developments related to the company are almost immediately reflected in the share price. In other words, the share price and the intrinsic value are continually the same.

At first glance, the EMH seems a preposterous theory. It would suggest that investors should simply look to track the market through ETFs and give up on attempting to beat the average market return. This is a difficult pill to swallow for proponents of fundamental analysis, who may spend hours of research looking for trends and patterns in the financial statements published by companies. Yet, studies have demonstrated support for the EMH in that price movements over the short term appear to be random. Investors consistently show an inability to identify undervalued stocks. Supporters of fundamental analysis are inclined to fire back that the share price converges towards intrinsic value over the long run, which is why investors are often encouraged to let their investment approach take effect over a minimum time period of 5 years or more.

Fundamental Analysis: Application

The theoretical debate between fundamental analysis and the EMH has still not been settled. Be that as it may, we have included some of the techniques that are used in fundamental analysis here to give you an insight into this strategy. If they interest you then this will provide a good start for further research. Otherwise, you may choose to adopt the EMH, which suggests that ETFs are your best bet.

Financial Statements & Ratio Analysis

In order to begin applying fundamental analysis, you must first be introduced to the financial statements. Each financial year, publicly-listed companies are obliged to publish an Annual Report that summarizes their financial activity for that year. This report can be found on the 'Investor Relations' webpage of all publicly-listed companies. Within this report, a section will be dedicated to the company's financial statements. We present the three most important here.

Income Statement (Statement of Profit & Loss)

This shows the income and expenses.

Balance Sheet (Statement of Financial Position)

This shows the assets (what you own) and liabilities (what you owe).

Cash Flow Statement

This shows the cash that enters and leaves the bank account.

The data that will be required to perform your own fundamental analysis on a company of your choice will be sourced from these statements. As the information presented in these formats can be hard to digest, especially when comparing between financial years, investors are able to provide an overview of the most prevalent information by using investment ratios. These ratios are split into the following five categories:

Profitability - shows how well expenses compare to income

Efficiency - shows how productively the company is using its assets

Liquidity - shows the company's ability to pay back what it owes

Leverage - shows how much debt the company has

Investment - shows the share price compared to competitors

The number of ratios that have been created by investors could be the subject of an entirely separate book. As this chapter serves to simply introduce you to the field of fundamental analysis, we have limited our examples to one ratio for each of the above-mentioned categories.

Profitability

For profitability, we will look at how to calculate the operating margin. This is calculated as the earnings before interest and tax (EBIT) divided by total revenue, expressed as a percentage. The EBIT figure can be found on the Income Statement and is often called the operating profit. This is your net profit for the financial year. Revenue is also found on the Income Statement; it is the top line, also known as total sales or total income.

We shall illustrate this calculation with an example. If Company A has made total revenue of $100 million USD in the financial year and an EBIT figure of $10 million USD, then we can calculate the operation margin as follows:

($10 million USD / $100 million USD) x 100% = 10%

Company A therefore has an operating margin of 10% in this financial year.

Efficiency

For efficiency, we will look at how to calculate the total asset turnover ratio. This number shows how well assets are being used to generate income for the company. A higher ratio is favorable. A ratio of 0.75 indicates that for every dollar worth of assets that the company owns, $0.75 USD of sales are being generated. It is calculated by dividing total revenue, which is found on the Income Statement, by total assets, which is found on the Balance Sheet.

We shall illustrate this calculation with an example. If Company A has made total revenue of $100 million USD in the financial year and owns $2oo million USD in total assets, then we can calculate the total asset turnover ratio as follows:

($100 million USD / $200 million USD) = 0.50

Company A therefore has a total asset turnover ratio of 0.5 in this financial year.

Liquidity

For liquidity, we will look at how to calculate the net cash position. Companies do not present their net cash position on the financial statements. Instead, they present their total cash position under assets, which is found on the Balance Sheet and their total debt position under liabilities, which is also found on the Balance Sheet. The net cash position can then be calculated by subtracting the total company debt from the total cash amount.

We shall illustrate this calculation with an example. If Company A has a total cash position of $20 million USD in the financial year and total debt of $5 million USD, then we can calculate the net cash position as follows:

$20 million USD - $5 million USD = $15 million USD

Company A therefore has a net cash position of $15 million USD in this financial year.

Leverage

For leverage, we will look at how to calculate the debt to equity ratio. This ratio can show the capital structure of a company. It displays how reliant a company is on debt funding. The higher the ratio, the more reliant the company is on debt funding. Shareholder equity is the amount remaining when total liabilities are subtracted from total assets, both of which are presented on the Balance Sheet. Total debt is also displayed on the Balance Sheet. The debt to equity ratio is then calculated by dividing total debt by the total shareholder equity figure.

We shall illustrate this calculation with an example. If Company A has a total shareholder equity figure of $100 million USD in the financial year and total debt of $200 million USD, then we can calculate the debt to equity ratio as follows:

$$(\$200 \text{ million USD} / \$100 \text{ million USD}) = 2.0$$

Company A therefore has a debt to equity ratio of 2.0 in this financial year.

Investment

For investment, we will look at how to calculate the price-earnings (P/E) ratio. The P/E ratio is a very important valuation metric in investment. It is calculated by dividing the share price by the earning per share (EPS) - which is presented on the Income Statement.

We shall illustrate this calculation with an example. If Company A has a current share price of $10 USD and has just reported earnings of $2 USD per share, then we can calculate the P/E ratio as follows:

$$(\$10 \text{ USD} / \$2 \text{ USD}) = 5.0$$

Company A therefore has a P/E ratio of 5.0 in this financial year. Put another way, it would take 5 years of earnings at the current rate for the investor to recoup his/her investment per share.

Now that you are familiar with how to calculate some of the most important financial ratios for a company, we will look at how these figures can be used to perform fundamental analysis. Ratios on there own do not possess much value. However, when compared to the ratios of competing companies or compared to the ratios of past years for the same company, trends in the data may be analyzed. This is the crux of fundamental analysis.

Let us take the P/E ratio as an important example. If you calculate that Company A has a current P/E ratio of 5.0, on its own that does not do you much good. Although, if you know that Company B is a competitor and has similar operations to Company A, then you may calculate that it has a P/E ratio of

10.0. By comparing these figures, it would take 5 years to recoup your investment in Company A but 10 years to recoup your investment in Company B. This may be an indicator that Company A is better value for your money than Company B.

Similarly, if you know that Company A operates in the US technology market sector, you can find out the average P/E ratio for the US technology sector through an internet search. Let us assume that it is 15. If the average P/E ratio for similar companies to Company A is 15 and Company A only has a P/E ratio of 5, then Company A starts to appear undervalued from this basic fundamental analysis. Of course, fair warning should be given that one metric alone should not be the basis for making an investment. Nonetheless, these financial ratios may be used to paint a picture that aids you in comparing one company against another based on its financial statements. This is the practical application of fundamental analysis.

Key Learning Points

- Fundamental analysis and the EMH are competing schools of thought for modern investment approaches
- Fundamental analysis looks to find trends in the financial statements of companies in order to identify undervalued and overvalued companies
- The EMH suggests that researching company values is a waste of time; the value of the company is shown as the share price multiplied by the number of shares issued
- The main financial statements are the Income Statement, the Balance Sheet and the Cash Flow Statement
- Financial ratios can be broken down into measures of profitability, efficiency, liquidity, leverage and investment

Chapter 7 - Alternative Investment Options

All new investors are excited to get started in the markets. Unfortunately, if this excitement is not guided appropriately, you may be tempted to run before you walk. We have often stated that investment requires self-discipline. The self-discipline to learn a practical investment approach and implement it slowly over time as you become more confident in your own investment competence. The common thread through each chapter so far has been our recommendation to begin investing through ETFs. These are relatively simple investment vehicles that can allow you to form a portfolio across the four main asset classes: equities, bonds, commodities and property. Naturally, the world of investment possibilities does extend beyond these asset classes to more esoteric options.

In this chapter, we will look at some of the alternative investment options available to investors and suggest why these are better suited for sophisticated investors. We provide information on volatility, cryptocurrencies and derivatives in this chapter so that you may be aware of them but these are specialized fields of investment. We recommend that you spend the time to become comfortable with an investment approach founded on using ETFs beyond venturing into these alternatives.

Volatility

Volatility has emerged over the last two decades as a new tradeable asset class. It is simply a measure of the fluctuation in market price of a given asset over a period of time. The most popular index for volatility is known as the VIX and it is measured by the Chicago Board Options Exchange (CBOE) in the US. The index measures the predicted volatility of the S&P 500 (a measure of the US stock market) over the next 30 days. Volatility can be split into historical volatility and implied volatility. Historical volatility is the actual movement of an asset over a past time period; implied volatility is the predicted movement of an asset over a future time period. Therefore, the VIX is a measure of implied volatility for the US stock market. If the volatility (VIX) level of the S&P 500 is 15.00, this means that the market is expected to move within a range of ± 15% over the next year, 68% of the time. This is a concept known as standard deviation in statistics, otherwise called the expected move.

ETFs have now appeared on the market that allow investors to trade the volatility level, as measured by the VIX. Another name for the VIX index is the 'fear indicator.' This name has been coined because when the S&P 500 index, which measures the US stock market, falls in value, the VIX almost always expands. So, in a falling stock market, when investors begin to panic sell, it is common to see the VIX increase - hence the name. An increasing VIX is an indicator of fear in the markets. As a new investor, this may be a good signal for you to look at buying equities. When the VIX increases, it is probable that the US stock market has just decreased. This presents you with an opportunity to buy shares at a cheaper price.

Cryptocurrencies

The latest rage in investment revolves around cryptocurrencies. In late 2008, Bitcoin emerged as the best-known example of this new asset class. While the details behind how the technology works can be complicated to understand, it is worth understanding a simplified form. Cryptocurrencies are effectively alternative money systems, allowing transactions to take place - exchanging a set number of the cryptocurrency for goods and services. Uniquely, these are decentralized digital cash systems that do not require a central entity to manage them. While currencies such as the USD require a central bank, the Federal Reserve, to authenticate which transactions are legitimate or counterfeit, cryptocurrencies have found a way around this by forming a peer-to-peer network. Instead of having a centralized database of transactions, blockchain technology is used to irreversibly embed a record of all authenticated purchases and sales using the currency into the currency itself. In this way, every user of the currency is instantly presented with a record of all other authentic transactions. This is then used to confirm the balance of all users in the cryptocurrency network.

Leaving the complexity of cryptocurrencies aside, let us examine their investment case as a potential new asset class. Firstly, cryptocurrencies trade on an electronic market and each one has an asset price. However, they do not generate an income for the user. This means that they are non-productive assets. Furthermore, the main reason why cryptocurrencies have risen to the attention of the investing world is that they have seen monumental increases in price since their emergence over the last decade. We would encourage you to reflect on why these prices have increased so drastically... Their price behavior shows a lot of signs of speculation; buyers buying for the sake of buying, in the hope that the price will continue to increase and they can sell for a profit. This is not investment as we have aimed to set out in this book. This is akin to gambling. If you wish to involve yourself in this investment frenzy then realize that the risk of losing your funds is very high. Speculation works until it doesn't. If cryptocurrencies are experiencing an asset bubble, which their price behavior seems to indicate, then the impending crash to the downside will take a lot of unsuspecting beginners by surprise. We would urge you to steer clear!

Derivatives (Options & Futures)

Derivatives are split into options and futures. They are named appropriately as they derive their value from the price of the underlying asset. Often times these are equities but derivatives also exist for bonds and commodities. Options and futures are contracts to buy or sell an asset at a predefined point in the future. The difference between them being that an option implies choice, whereas futures contracts are obligatory - they do not present the buyer or seller with choice.

Futures allow traders to make arrangements to buy or sell an asset in the future. This serves a useful industrial function as farmers, to pick an example, may wish to fix the selling price of their crops months in advance of the harvest. Meanwhile, speculators may wish to take the other side of the contract because they believe that the price of the crops will increase by the time the harvest comes around. In this way, a contract can be established now to buy and sell a set quantity of crops at a point in the future. A future price must be used, which is set by the futures market, and both parties cannot back out of the contract once established. The only way to exit the contract is to take the opposite side of the future in the market. A buyer of a future must sell the contract in the market to close his/her position; vice-versa applies to the seller of a future, who must buy the contract in the market to close his/her position. If the future price has moved favorably, then trading futures like this can present an opportunity to profit. Equally, if the price has moved unfavorably then the speculator can also lose money.

Options work in a similar fashion. Buyers of options pay the seller to have the right - but not the obligation - to buy or sell an asset at a set price at a predefined time in the future. Call options give the buyer the right to buy an asset at a set price; put options give the buyer the right to sell an asset at a set price. Unlike futures, the buyer does not have to exercise his/her option contract. Let us take the example of an option contract on an ounce of gold. Let us assume the current price for an ounce of gold is $1,000. We now buy a call option for 3 months' time at a price of $1,100. We will have to pay the seller of the option contract for this right. In 3 months' time, assume that the price of gold has now increased to $1,200 per ounce. We can exercise our option contract to obligate the seller to sell us an ounce of gold at our contract price - $1,100. We can then choose to sell our ounce of gold on the market for $1,200, realizing a $100 profit. Alternatively, we can say that our option contract is worth $100. However, if the price of gold had actually fallen to $900 per ounce, it would not have made sense for us to exercise our option contract. Why would we make the seller of the contract sell us an ounce of gold at $1,100 when we can buy it on the market at $900? This is where an option contract would benefit us over a future. A future would force us to exercise the contract and we would realize a $200 loss. In this case though, we would only have lost the original amount that the seller charged us for establishing the option contract.

Key Learning Points

- Volatility is a new asset class; the VIX 'fear indicator' generally increases when the US market S&P 500 falls, presenting you with a potential buying opportunity for equities
- Cryptocurrencies display the pricing behavior of a speculative bubble; we would recommend that you avoid them completely
- Derivatives allow investors to trade assets using future prices for a predetermined time point in the future

Chapter 8 - Investment Strategies: Need to Know

Now you are beginning to make progress on your investment journey. We have covered each of the main asset classes and made you aware of your own risk tolerance level. Here comes the fun part: putting it all together! All investors manage what is known as a portfolio of investments. This is a combination of all the different asset classes that the investor has put his/her savings into. In this chapter, we will look at some potential portfolio setups with the asset allocation chosen to match each of the 3 risk tolerance levels.

Diversification

You may have seen us make mention of diversification throughout this book. That is because it is a fundamental investment approach that is used to reduce the overall risk of your portfolio. It simply means that instead of having all your eggs in one basket, you should spread them out between asset classes. The percentage split of your asset allocation should be chosen with your risk tolerance and wealth objectives in mind. If you are in your 20s and 30s looking to make as much money as possible and have a risk-seeking attitude, it would make little sense to put all of your portfolio into bonds. This is where the knowledge that you have accumulated in this book will help guide you to an appropriate investment selection.

Hedging

Diversification is similar to the principle of hedging risk. This is where assets are placed in your portfolio that are known to move inversely to each other; as one goes up in price, the other generally goes down in price. This is a relationship that is widely accepted to exist between the stock market and bonds. Equities and precious metals (such as gold) are also partners that are commonly used in hedging strategies. You may wonder why would you want to pursue an investment approach that limits your upside in this way? The answer is that diversification and hedging minimize the risk of your overall portfolio. If all asset markets were to go in the same direction against you, this would expose you to large potential losses without employing these strategies.

Portfolio Construction

Risk-Averse

We have already established that risk-averse investors are often already in retirement or are approaching retirement. The key wealth objective of this group is to preserve wealth, rather than grow it, and to maximize income. Exposure to risk should therefore be kept minimal in the portfolio for this investor profile. As we have advocated the use of ETFs and REITs for beginning investors throughout this book, the portfolios constructed here assume that only these investment vehicles are to be employed.

Let us first recap the four main asset classes and the unique traits of each. This will help to reaffirm why certain asset classes are best suited to different risk-tolerance levels.

Equities: shares that give the investor rights to company dividends

Bonds: debt that entitles the bondholder to interest payments

Commodities: 'hard' and 'soft' materials that generate no income

Property: residential and commercial that generate rental income

As risk-averse investors are most interested in income, we can already rule out commodities as an inappropriate asset class due to them being non-productive. While some investors may advocate that no equities should be held in a portfolio for this risk category, we would suggest that some exposure to the stock market is optional. Equities do provide an income through dividend payments, yet share prices are known to fluctuate more than bonds or property prices on average. With this in mind, we would suggest keeping exposure to equities below 25% of your overall portfolio allocation. Instead, the portfolio should be weighted towards bonds which provide more stability in price and expected income. Our example portfolio asset allocation could therefore look as follows:

Equities - up to 25%

Bonds - 50%

Commodities - 0%

Property - 25%

Risk-Neutral

Next, we turn our attention to the portfolio construction of a risk-neutral investor. While this investor may be somewhat indifferent to risk exposure, it still appears sensible to stay away from commodities. This is an asset class associated with large price swings and would be best avoided by those not actively seeking to take risk with their investment approach. In order to gain exposure to some upside potential, though, a risk-neutral investor should put a substantial proportion of his/her portfolio into equities. This investor profile is often in midlife, with the wealth objective of growing his/her retirement fund or growing an investment fund for the purposes of funding a child's education plan. As the investor seeks to grow wealth, equities shall provide the driver to meet this objective. The remaining portfolio fund can then be split evenly between bonds and property, which follows the sensible approach of diversification and hedges some of the risk associated with the stock market exposure. Our example portfolio asset allocation could therefore look as follows:

Equities - 50%

Bonds - 25%

Commodities - 0%

Property - 25%

Risk-Taker

At the opposite end of the spectrum, we find the risk-seeking investor. This investor profile is often young, in his/her 20s and 30s, and has the wealth objective of rapidly increasing his/her savings. Bonds and property are both ill-suited asset classes to meet this aim, as they demonstrate traits of minimal price movement. This investor must expose the portfolio to larger risk of loss than the alternative risk tolerance groups, with the intention to benefit from large upwards price movements. Equities and commodities both fit this need. Our example portfolio asset allocation could therefore look as follows:

Equities - 75%

Bonds - 0%

Commodities - 25%

Property - 0%

Variations

While we have set out potential portfolio constructions for each risk tolerance group, we have focused broadly on the percentage split between the four main asset classes. This means that you may experiment with the multitude of various ETFs available on the market and make the portfolio your own. We maintain that there is no better way to learn about investment than through practical experience. Explore the different equity ETFs between developed and emerging markets, different geographical locations, market sectors and company capitalizations. Remember to keep your portfolio balanced and if the percentage split begins to move out of your comfort zone, then you are always able to adjust your positions by selling part of your overweight asset class and buying some more of the underweight asset class. Investors are not speculators. You must allow time to work in your favor; once you have set up your investment portfolio, monitor it but do not adjust it too frequently. Our recommended time horizon would be a minimum of 3 years, but 5 years and upwards is preferable.

Key Learning Points

- Diversification means not putting all of your investment fund into one asset class; hedging risk means investing in asset classes that often move in opposite directions to each other
- Risk-averse investors should prioritize income; the portfolio should be weighted towards bonds and property
- Risk-neutral investors require some exposure to the stock market; the portfolio should be split with a slight weighting towards equities
- Risk-seeking investors require the benefits of asset classes with large price fluctuations in order to maximize their likelihood of making large gains; the portfolio should be weighted towards equities and commodities

Conclusion

This book was written with the intention of introducing beginners to the world of investment. We have covered the different risk tolerances that sit at the heart of a well-planned investment approach. You should now be able to identify your own investor profile and have a clearer idea of your wealth objectives. Gaining clarity on these points is essential to developing a coherent investment strategy. We have also discussed the theoretical debate taking place within academia between fundamental analysis and the Efficient Market Hypothesis (EMH). As a beginner, it can be useful to have a conceptual overview of ratio analysis, which we have touched upon, if you seek to value individual companies. However, it is certainly not necessary to achieve success in investment.

We have also discovered the key asset classes: equities, bonds, commodities and property. These are each best suited to different risk tolerance levels and we would urge you to recap our suggested portfolio constructions. Exchange Traded Funds (ETFs) offer a versatile solution to new investors and we would recommend that you incorporate them in your own investment approach as you build your portfolio. These investment vehicles allow you to invest across a basket of equities by geographical location, market sector and company capitalization. They can also give you exposure to the bond market and a range of commodities. Similarly, Real Estate Investment Trusts (REITs) can allow you to add residential or commercial property as an additional asset class to your balanced portfolio.

It is our hope that this book will serve as a platform to launch your investment journey. There is no doubt that the world of investment can be overwhelming to the uninitiated. That is why we have set out practical steps for improvement and summarized our Key Learning Points at the end of each chapter. If ever you need to recap the crucial lessons from this book, you can use these sections to refresh your memory. Keep in mind that not all assets will be suitable for you as you start out; volatility, derivatives and cryptocurrencies are three examples that we would advise you to avoid until you develop your investment competence.

Our path together now comes to an end but we hope your investment journey has only just begun. All that is left for us to say is best of luck and have fun out there in the markets!

Disclaimer

The information contained in **"HOW TO INVEST IN THE STOCK MARKET - Secrets Of The World's Best Stock Market Investors"** and its components, is meant to serve as a comprehensive collection of strategies that the author of this eBook has done research about. Summaries, strategies, tips and tricks are only recommendations by the author, and reading this eBook will not guarantee that one's results will exactly mirror the author's results.

The author of this Ebook has made all reasonable efforts to provide current and accurate information for the readers of this eBook. The author and its associates will not be held liable for any unintentional errors or omissions that may be found.

The material in the Ebook may include information by third parties. Third party materials comprise of opinions expressed by their owners. As such, the author of this eBook does not assume responsibility or liability for any third party material or opinions.

The publication of third party material does not constitute the author's guarantee of any information, products, services, or opinions contained within third party material. Use of third party material does not guarantee that your results will mirror our results. Publication of such third party material is simply a recommendation and expression of the author's own opinion of that material.

Whether because of the progression of the Internet, or the unforeseen changes in company policy and editorial submission guidelines, what is stated as fact at the time of this writing may become outdated or inapplicable later.

This Ebook is copyright ©2018 by **Richard Nolan** with all rights reserved. It is illegal to redistribute, copy, or create derivative works from this Ebook whole or in parts. No parts of this report may be reproduced or retransmitted in any forms whatsoever without the written expressed and signed permission from the author.